Rubbish

Gill Tanner

Photographs by Maggie Murray

Illustrations by Sheila Jackson

Contents

A & C Black · London

What do we throw away?

Each month the average ▶ household throws away about 72 kilos of rubbish. Three-quarters of it is packaging.

Every day we throw away rubbish. This picture shows some of the rubbish found on a modern rubbish tip. You can probably spot used packaging, waste food, newspapers, old clothes and worn-out shoes. What kinds of rubbish do you throw out of your home?

Advertisements encourage us to buy 'new, better and improved goods' of all kinds. They try to convince us that we ought to have the same possessions as everyone else. But everything we buy produces more rubbish. Have you ever thought what happens to all our rubbish?

Rubbish from your great ► grandparents' day. They threw away far less than we do, partly because they were less wasteful, and partly because there was far less packaging in those days.

When your great grandparents were children, only a few very rich people could afford to fill their houses with possessions. Most people were too poor to own much. Wages were lower than they are now and many people were unemployed. There were also fewer things for people to buy, so there was less to throw away.

Most poor families had to 'make ends meet' by mending and reusing everything they possibly could. They would have been shocked at the amount of rubbish we throw away so carelessly.

SEE that NOTHING is THROWN AWAY WHICH might HAVE SERVED YOUR FAMILY OR A POORER ONE

3

Time-line

	Great great grandparents were born			Great grandparents were born		
	pre-1880s	1880s	1890s	1900s	1910s	1920s
Important events	**1870** Alexander Graham Bell invents telephone	**1888** Dunlop invents pneumatic tyre	**1890** Moving pictures start **1896** First modern Olympic Games	**1901** Queen Victoria dies. Edward VII becomes King **1903** Wright brothers fly first plane	**1910** George V becomes King **1914–18** World War I	**1926** General Strike in Britain
Rubbish dates	**1872** Compulsory Medical Officers of Health appointed to advise all town councils on matters concerning the health of the people **1875** Public Health Act forced all town councils to introduce rubbish collections **1876** First refuse destructor erected in Manchester ● River Pollution Prevention Act made dumping rubbish in rivers illegal	**1882** Robert Koch identifies the bacillus (germ) which causes cholera **1883** First portable galvanised iron dustbin introduced	**1892** Penny in the slot gas meters made gas fires more convenient to use. Wider use of gas fires and cookers meant more unburnt rubbish **1897** Workman's Compensation Act. Injured workers were no longer left penniless, so they were less likely to scavenge	**1908** Old age pension. Old people no longer had to scavenge to survive	**1911** Unemployment assistance. Money paid to people out of work so they were no longer forced to scavenge	**1922** Uncontrolled dumping of rubbish made illegal **1926** Electric National Grid. More electric fires meant less rubbish was burnt

4

This time-line shows some of the important events since your great great grandparents were children and some of the events and inventions which have changed our rubbish and the way we dispose of it.

Parents were born
You were born

930s	1940s	1950s	1960s	1970s	1980s	1990s
Edward ibdicates rge VI imes King rst /ision idcasts	**1941** Penicillin successfully tested	**1952** Elizabeth II becomes Queen		**1973** Britain enters the Common Market	**1981** First successful space shuttle flight	
World II starts	**1945** World War II ends **1947** First supersonic plane	EIIR **1959** Yuri Gagarin first man in space	**1969** Neil Armstrong first man on the moon			
Means ed istance. ple iting state stance had ell their iables ire they id receive money	**1940** Collections of metal, paper, rubber and food scraps became vital for the war effort. Saving waste became patriotic and everyone did it	**1950s** Polythene household articles became popular	**1960** Increasing amounts of paper and plastic packaging used		**1985** Start of privatisation of refuse collections. Some local authorities handed their refuse collections over to private companies	**1990** First plant for recycling polythene bags into new bags and black bin liners opened in Derbyshire. Cardiff became the second recycling city
	1945 Family Allowance Benefit. Mothers received money for their children from the state.				**1989** Sheffield became the first recycling city by adopting many new recycling schemes for its rubbish ● In this year the average family in the UK threw away 624 family-sized plastic drinks bottles, 6 trees worth of paper and 600 metal cans	

5

Feeding off rubbish: nature's dustmen

Some of great grandma's rubbish was eaten by animals. In the country, food scraps were given to the chickens and pigs. Until a few years ago pig-breeders collected vegetable, fish and meat waste from shops.

Other animals which lived off rubbish were less welcome, especially the vermin which ate, and bred in rubbish. Flora Klickman, in her book *Mistress of the Little House* (1902), wrote:

'... there is nothing more certain to ensure sickness in the household than neglected garbage ... it encourages rats and mice, which may in turn run over food indoors, and in this way bring typhus germs to the family ...'

▲ Rats like to nest in rubbish. Your great grandparents may have set traps for the rats and mice, or called in the rat catcher and his dog to do it for them. Modern pest controllers mostly use poison.

Household pests

In 1849, 53,000 people died during an epidemic of cholera in Britain. This shocking event persuaded the government to take action to improve sewage and rubbish disposal in overcrowded cities. By the turn of the century, thanks to the work of scientists like Louis Pasteur, most people knew that the dirt and germs which caused disease could be carried by pests.

A kitchen range. Burning ▶ rubbish saved buying so much wood or coal and turned the rubbish into ash which did not rot or smell. The ashes could be used for cleaning saucepans or even teeth!

People were advised to burn on the kitchen range anything which might create a health hazard or encourage vermin, including old bones and used tins. The ashes, and anything which had not burned, then went into the dustbin. The range was also used for cooking, warming the house and heating water.

◀ The Demon beetle trap, fly paper and crochet lace covers for the milk jug and sugar basin helped to control pests.

Dustmen

Machinery inside a modern refuse lorry squashes the rubbish so that it takes up less space. This means that each lorry can collect a huge amount of rubbish, but it is difficult to separate glass,aluminium or paper which could be recycled.

Today the local council arranges the removal of rubbish from our streets and homes. We don't want rubbish heaps rotting near our houses, so many people put their refuse into plastic bags to keep the flies out and the smells in.

At the turn of the century, dust carts were pulled ▶ by horses which were trained to stand still while the dustmen climbed the ladder to empty the heavy bins. The high sides stopped the rubbish from blowing away.

Refuse collectors usually collect household rubbish once a week. Larger items, such as beds and cookers, which are too big to go into a bin can be collected by arrangement with the council or taken to the tips or dumps the council must provide. Each adult pays towards these services in their taxes.

During the early part of Queen Victoria's reign much ill health was caused by polluted rivers and drinking water, and by rotting rubbish near people's homes. Sometimes these illnesses became epidemics. Hundreds or even thousands of people living in dirty, overcrowded conditions caught diseases from each other and died.

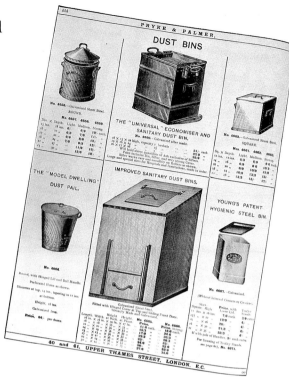

▲ This advertisement of 1900 shows several types of dustbin which were in use at the time. Most were made from galvanised metal which did not rust.

In 1872 Medical Officers of Health were appointed to advise councils about health in their area. They persuaded councils to start regular rubbish collections. Householders were each given an ash bin, tub or pail for all their waste. Some councils provided carbolic disinfectant which was sprinkled into the empty bins to kill germs.

Most people kept their bin outside their back door. If they lived in terraced houses, they would be woken up by the dustmen who needed to walk through the house to reach the bin in the back yard.

Where does the rubbish go?

Some modern refuse is destroyed in huge incinerators which burn rubbish at high temperatures. Once the refuse lorries dump their loads into containers ready to feed the furnace, only metals which are magnetic can be separated for recycling. Everything else is reduced to ash and clinker.

However, not all rubbish burns well and incinerators can cause air pollution, so most modern rubbish is buried in landfill sites. These are big holes in the ground filled with layers of squashed refuse and earth. Here organic rubbish, such as kitchen waste and paper, starts to rot. Bacteria help it to break down and disappear. Other types of refuse, such as glass and some types of plastic, won't rot and never disappear.

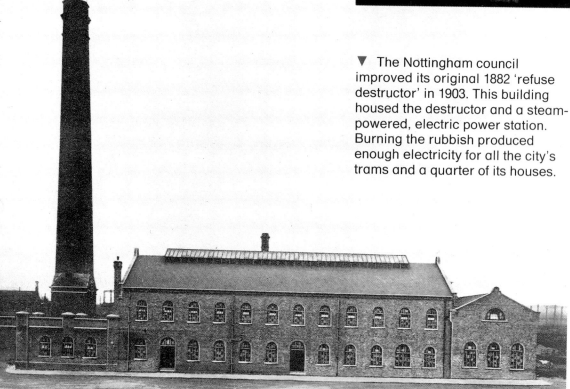

▼ The Nottingham council improved its original 1882 'refuse destructor' in 1903. This building housed the destructor and a steam-powered, electric power station. Burning the rubbish produced enough electricity for all the city's trams and a quarter of its houses.

◀ A council waste tip. Some rubbish is dumped on tips like these before being taken away for incineration or to a landfill site. Each year the British people throw away millions of pounds worth of materials which could be recycled, including 5,000,000 glass bottles, nearly 2,000,000 tonnes of paper and 5,000,000,000 aluminium drinks cans each worth 1p. We could save energy and raw materials if we separated the reusable materials for recycling.

▼ This picture, drawn in 1873, shows a city dust yard. One dust yard on the banks of the Regent Canal in London employed over 100 men and women to pick through the rubbish.

Town councils at the turn of the century expected the rubbish to pay for the costs of the men, horses and carts used to collect it. Once the rubbish had been collected, it was dumped at a dust yard to be sorted.

Anything useful was salvaged. Whatever was left which could rot or burn was taken to an incinerator or to a rubbish dump. The clinker from the incinerator was used for road-mending or sold to be ground up for mortar.

11

Making money from rubbish

▲ This poster shows how people were encouraged to salvage and sell any useful rubbish.

Have you ever saved certain types of rubbish to raise money? Charities collect used postage stamps, silver foil, aluminium cans and newspapers. These are sold for recycling and the money put to good use.

At the turn of the century salvaging and recycling were much more common than they are now. People did not save their rubbish for charities, they sold it for money to survive.

Even those families who were slightly better off salvaged and sold their rubbish. The money they raised was used to give them special treats.

Scavengers
1. 'Bone grubbers' searched the streets and rubbish heaps for scraps of bone.
2. Children collected horse manure to sell as garden fertiliser.
3. Workers sieved rubbish at dust yards to salvage anything valuable.
4. 'Mudlarks' searched river beds at low tide.
5. 'Toshers' searched the sewers.

SOAP WORKS

4

5

Some poor people worked as scavengers, rummaging through other people's rubbish in search of anything they could sell. Many scavengers were children, or old or ill. There were no pensions or National Health Service, and the only place where they could go for help was the workhouse. Here they were given basic food and clothing, but they had to obey strict rules, and do hard, boring work to pay for their keep. Most people feared these grim places and would do any work, however dirty or unhealthy, to avoid going there.

Imagine scavenging through modern litter. What might be worth salvaging?

Travelling collectors

A hundred years ago, housewives sold a lot of rubbish to travelling collectors who went from house to house. These men then sold what they collected to rag and bottle shops, or, in the case of larger items, to scrap dealers. The dealers had shops and yards where they stored the rubbish before selling it to industries to be recycled.

The street cry 'Rags and bones. Any old rags and bones!' or the sound of a bell would have encouraged people to bring out old clothes, bottles, jars, meat-bones and scrap metals. The rag and bone man would pay very small prices, but people were glad to be rid of their rubbish and pleased with even a few extra pennies to help with the housekeeping.

Mrs Norton, who was a child in London at the turn of the century, remembers:

'The rag and bone man gave an old half-penny for four empty jam jars. Sometimes you got a goldfish instead of money. The man kept them in a bucket on the cart. You kept the fish in another jam jar'.

◀ A rag and bone man pushing his barrow through the richer streets of a town.

◀ Rag and bottle shops, such as the one shown in this contemporary picture, smelled disgusting because the rubbish in them was not washed. The outside of the shops were often painted bright colours so that old or feeble-minded scavengers could find them. Many very poor people bought their clothes at shops like these.

▲ These toys, curling tongs and other metal items from the turn of the century might have been sold as scrap metal or even made from recycled metal.

'Any old iron?' was the street-cry of any dealer who came round buying scrap metal. The scrap metal dealer sorted the scrap into the different types of metal, waiting until he had a full load to sell to the smelting works to be melted down so the metal could be re-used.

There is still a thriving business in scrap ▶ metal. These children went to their local tip and sorted out the different types of metal. Each type went into a different skip. **Never** go to a tip without a grown up, they can be very dangerous places.

Shopping and packaging

Many of us buy food ready weighed and packaged from large, self-service supermarkets. At the turn of the century most people used much smaller shops, some of which sold only one type of food such as meat, fish or bread.

▼ This grocer's shop displayed its home-cured hams and bacon by hanging them in the street. Rich people could place their orders and the goods would be taken to their homes by a delivery boy with a horse and cart or a bicycle.

Most food was served out of its original sack, barrel, tin or box. The shop assistant weighed and packed the goods into exactly the amounts the customer wanted. Butter and cheese were cut from large blocks. Sugar was cut from a solid sugar 'loaf'. The purchases were wrapped in paper bags, brown paper, or newspaper and string, which great grandma saved, reused or burnt.

▼ These children visited Brewhouse Yard Museum in Nottingham to see a grocer's shop which had been reconstructed using furniture and equipment from the turn of the century. Notice the huge metal coffee grinder, the brass scales and the large pot for storing and serving lemonade.

▲ Modern packaging creates huge amounts of rubbish.

There were no sell-by dates, so instead of throwing away broken or stale food, shopkeepers sold it cheaply. Mrs Norton remembers that:

'... a treat was a pennyworth of broken biscuits, you got more to eat than with a pennyworth of sweets. If you were lucky you might get a nearly whole one or a cream-filled one ...'.

Three-quarters of our rubbish is paper, plastic, cardboard, polystyrene, glass or metal packaging. At the turn of the century, manufacturers didn't use so much bright packaging. Tins, for example, had no paper wrapping round them. The labels were usually painted on the metal. White pottery had the maker's name printed on the surface, and the writing on bottles was moulded into the glass. Many containers could be returned to the shop. All this meant that great grandma had far less rubbish to throw away.

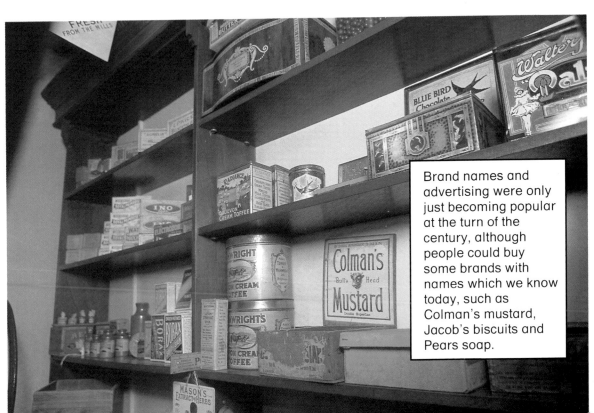

Brand names and advertising were only just becoming popular at the turn of the century, although people could buy some brands with names which we know today, such as Colman's mustard, Jacob's biscuits and Pears soap.

Clothes and rags

'If I'd as much money as I could tell,
I never would cry "Old clothes to sell,
Old clothes to sell, old clothes to sell".
I never would cry "Old clothes to sell".'

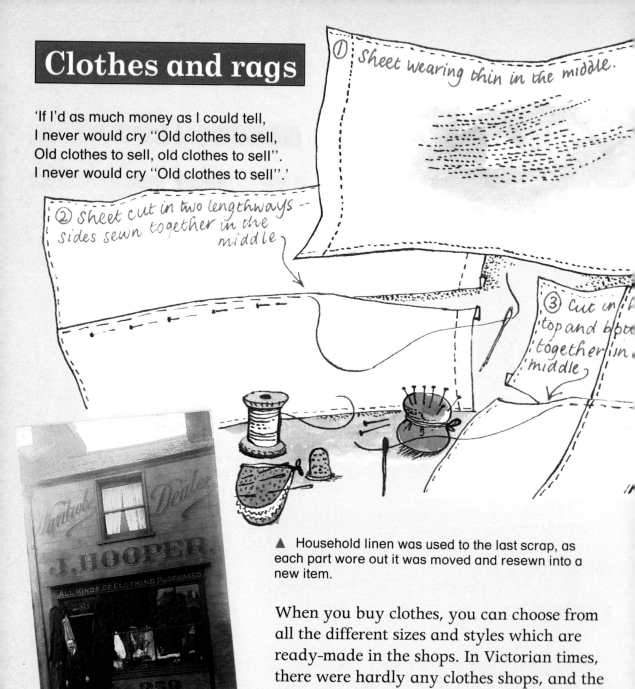

① Sheet wearing thin in the middle.

② Sheet cut in two lengthways – sides sewn together in the middle

③ cut in h top and bo together in middle

▲ Household linen was used to the last scrap, as each part wore out it was moved and resewn into a new item.

▲ The wardrobe dealer bought and sold second-hand clothes. His shop was very important for poor people because they could buy ready-to-wear garments, made of better material than they could otherwise afford.

When you buy clothes, you can choose from all the different sizes and styles which are ready-made in the shops. In Victorian times, there were hardly any clothes shops, and the few department stores were mainly in big cities. Most people made their clothes at home. They would go to a draper's shop to buy fabric, patterns, pins, needles and thread.

Women who were better off had the fabric they had chosen sent to a dressmaker. Wealthy gentlemen went to a tailor for made-to-measure suits.

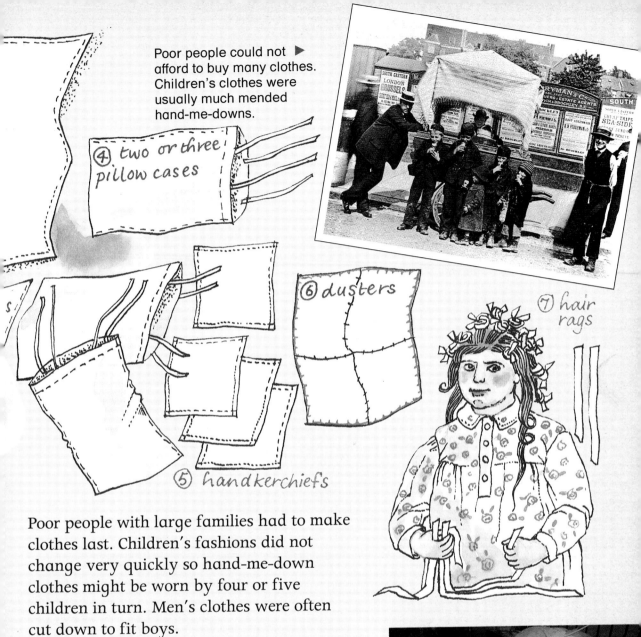

Poor people could not ▶ afford to buy many clothes. Children's clothes were usually much mended hand-me-downs.

④ two or three pillow cases

⑥ dusters

⑦ hair rags

s

⑤ handkerchiefs

Poor people with large families had to make clothes last. Children's fashions did not change very quickly so hand-me-down clothes might be worn by four or five children in turn. Men's clothes were often cut down to fit boys.

Great grandma might have used pieces from old shirts or blouses to make patchwork. Thicker scraps from worn-out coats and trousers were cut into strips and poked through old sacks to make 'peg' or 'rag' mats.

Large quantities of rags from rag and bone men or from rag and bottle shops were cleaned and shredded, then made into mattress filling, cheap poor-quality cloth or best-quality paper.

▲ These patchwork quilts were made in Victorian times.

19

Paper

Although we are starting to save more paper for recycling, most of it is thrown away. At the turn of the century, waste-paper shops bought old newspapers, magazines and comics in large bundles. The newspapers were made into cardboard, and the comics were re-sold, two for a half-penny.

Great grandma saved and reused all the paper bags, newspaper and brown paper from her parcels. Coloured pictures from magazines, postcards and greetings cards were stuck into scrap books or used to decorate bottles, boxes and screens.

▲ The children found this screen which had been decorated with pictures cut from Victorian magazines. Decorations made in this way are called découpage.

◀ Even letters were re-used. This unfinished piece of patchwork, from 1890, was made using paper templates cut from old letters and the pages of children's school exercise books.

Great grandma could not buy recycled paper, but she did re-use old newspaper in all sorts of ways, as these tips from a magazine of 1910 show:

Newspaper also had another use. Mrs Norton remembers:

'On Saturday mornings my job was to cut up the week's newspapers into six-inch squares, make holes in the corners with a carpet needle, and thread them on to loops of old string. These bundles were hung on a nail in the privy as toilet paper for the week'.

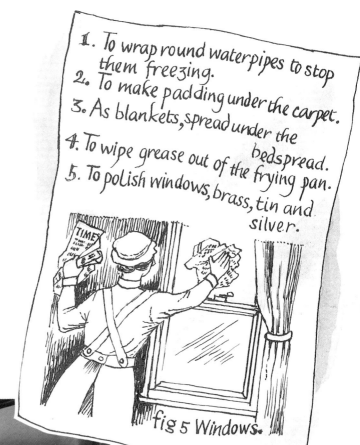

1. To wrap round waterpipes to stop them freezing.
2. To make padding under the carpet.
3. As blankets, spread under the bedspread.
4. To wipe grease out of the frying pan.
5. To polish windows, brass, tin and silver.

fig 5 Windows.

◀ The children cut out newspaper to make shelf decorations in exactly the same way that great grandma did.

Bottles and jars

Pot and stone bottles and jars. Most of them could be refilled and used again.

ginger beer

stove blacking

ink

cream

ECELSIOR·DAIRY·C&
·URE·RICH·CREAM

Carefully prepared from
the purest ingredients by
Boots
CASH CHEMISTS

CHERRY
TOOTH PASTE
Boots Cash
Chemists

L.R. NELSONS
IMPROVED INHALER
DIRECTIONS FOR USE
REMOVE MOUTHPIECE.HALF FILL INHALER
BOILING WATER.DROP REMEDY ON SPONGE
MOUTH-PIECE . APPLY LIPS TO IT.
BREATHE FREELY IN AND OUT AS IN ORDINARY
FULL RESPIRATION . WHEN ONLY THE VAPOUR
OF HOT WATER OR ANY INFUSION IS DESIRED
REMOVE THE SPONGE FROM MOUTHPIECE

ink   medicine   toothpaste   stove blacking   medicine inhaler

▼ We can put our old bottles into a bottle bank for recycling. All modern glass bottles and jars contain recycled glass.

Every week we throw away plastic and glass bottles and jars which once contained food or drink. People in Victorian times also bought many types of food and drink in bottles and jars. Most of these were made of glass, but some 'pot' or 'stone' bottles were made of heavy pottery or stoneware. Fizzy drinks, such as ginger beer, came in thick glass or stone bottles which wouldn't explode easily if the bottles were shaken.

Great grandma rarely threw away bottles. When she bought them the shop charged a small deposit which was repaid when the empty bottles were returned. The empties were then sterilised and re-filled, as with modern milk bottles.

Great grandma may have made her own lemonade and jam so she probably cleaned many bottles herself. The *London* magazine printed in 1910 suggested this method:

'. . . put the glass bottles into fine coal ashes and shake well, either with water or not, hot or cold according to the substance that fouls the bottle'.

Glass bottles and jars came in many different shapes and colours, which helped to identify the contents. Poison bottles were often hexagonal or triangular. Warnings such as 'Not to be taken' were pressed into the glass so that even blind people would not drink from them by mistake. Can you find any bottles in your home with words pressed into the glass?

▲ This reconstructed chemist's shop in Brewhouse Yard Museum, shows some of the bottles used at the turn of the century for perfume, pills, poisons and medicines.

◄ Glassware
1. medicine bottle
2. poison
3. disinfectant
4. bottle which had a marble stopper
5. torpedo bottle, which was kept on its side so the cork didn't dry out
6. eye-bath
7. baby's bottle

23

Bone and wood

You probably throw your old meat bones in the bin or give them to a dog. At the turn of the century bones were made into all kinds of useful objects, such as toothbrushes and buttons, many of which are now made from plastic. Usually the thick leg bones of horses or cattle were used. They had to be boiled for a long time to kill all the germs and to make sure the bones didn't smell or rot. Some people made a living out of boiling bones – a very smelly job.

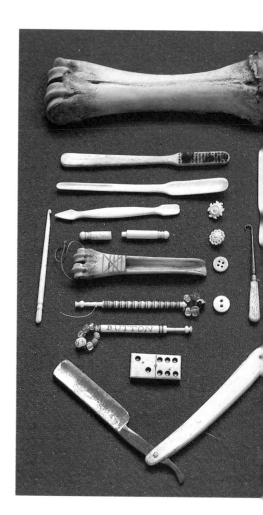

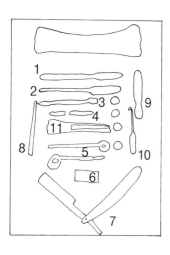

Bone objects from the ▶ turn of the century

1. toothbrush
2. bone-marrow scoop
3. manicure tool
4. needle case
5. lace bobbins
6. domino
7. cut-throat razor
8. crochet hook
9. letter opener
10. button hook, for doing up boot buttons
11. apple corer

Wood scraps could be sold for firewood, but were worth more money if they were carved or turned on a lathe to make lace bobbins, toys and buttons.

◀ Objects all made from wood at the turn of the century.

1. cup and ball game
2. pastry wheel
3. lace bobbins
4. buttons
5. needle cases
6. toy
7. opener for marble bottles
8. inkwell
9. spinning top

Hair

What do you do with the dead hair which collects in your brush or comb? Great grandma almost certainly kept her hair 'combings' in little crochet bags called hair-tidies that hung by the dressing table mirror. A hairdresser or wig-maker made the combings into false curls or ringlets for her. Since these hair pieces were made from her own hair, they looked natural.

These false curls were made by ▶ knotting lengths of thick hair on to a fine cord. The hairdresser curled the hair into ringlets which were then attached to a ribbon cap.

Some hairnets were also made from hair combings, so they were invisible when worn.

People often wore brooches or lockets with hair inside, a gift from a true love or in memory of someone who had died.

◀ These necklaces, earrings and watch-chain were cleverly made by knotting and weaving fine strands of human hair.

Menders

At the turn of the century, many household goods, such as irons and cookers, were advertised to 'last a lifetime'. If something did break, it was rarely thrown away. Household goods had few moving parts to wear out, so mending them was quite easy.

Shoes and boots were expensive and had to last a long time. The cobbler replaced worn leather soles and heels, and put metal 'segs' on the toes and heels to stop them wearing out so quickly. Poor families often stuffed newspapers or rags into their shoes when they could not afford to have them mended.

▲ In Victorian times most menders travelled around doing their repairs in the street.

▼ This girl visited a cobbler's shop at Brewhouse Yard Museum, Nottingham. The shop contains equipment and furniture which would have been used at the turn of the century. Can you spot the foot-shaped 'lasts' that fit inside the shoes being mended?

Some menders travelled around the country in all weather, offering their services. Many had special cries to attract customers, such as 'Any old chairs to mend' or 'Knives to grind'. They brought news from the places they visited, and often gossiped with the servants while they worked in the street.

▲ A tinker at work.

'Have you any work for a
  tinker, mistress?
Old brass, old pots, or kettles?
I'll mend them with a tink terry
  tink.
And never hurt your metals.'

▼ A knife grinder.

H SMITH.
TINMAN &
CUTLER.

▲ There are very few travelling menders left. This modern chair mender has his own workshop and people have to bring their chairs to him to be repaired.

Travelling menders carried their workshops and tools with them. The knife-grinder, for instance, brought his grinding wheel on a push cart. He pedalled with his feet to turn the grindstone, leaving his hands free to hold the knife blade steadily against the stone.

Learning from rubbish

Most of the things photographed for this book were rubbish. They were unwanted, worn out, or were replaced by new inventions. Many of them were found years later and then became important again.

Museums collect and display all sorts of objects that can teach us about people of the past, their inventions, and the changes that have taken place as a result. Some of these objects from the past are rare and valuable; others are beautiful, strange or funny. People collect and treasure them and they are not rubbish any more.

What could your great grandchildren learn about life today if they sorted through our rubbish?

Many scientists now believe that if we continue to make and use so many things, and then throw away millions of tons of rubbish, we will ruin the Earth. The only way we can make sure that our children have a happy future is to use less, throw away less and re-use many more things.

It seems, after all these years, that great grandma still has some useful lessons for us. What do you think we can learn from her?

These objects have all been found by members of a local history society in old rubbish tips.

◀ The children were allowed to help in a local history society dig. They found several old bottles and a lot of broken pottery.

Some of the bottles were ▶ in quite good condition. The children washed them carefully using ash and water which was the recommended method at the turn of the century. Once the bottles had been cleaned, they were examined for clues to show what they used to hold.

How to find out more

Start here	To find out about. . .	Who will have. . .
Old people	Their past	Memories of 'making ends meet', the rag and bone man, and street menders
Junk shops, flea markets and specialist old clothes shops	Old things to buy	Old packaging, old advertisements, old bottles and jars, things made of wood and paper, clothes from the past
● Local museums ● Natural history museums	● Packaging, everyday objects from the past ● Animals and pests which live off rubbish	● Reconstructed shops and rooms, displays of packaging, adverts, kitchen ranges and cookers. Displays of hair jewellery, things made out of bone and wood ● Loan collections. Lists of local collectors who might show their collections ● Displays and information on the lives and habits of scavengers
Local libraries	● Loans collections ● Reference collections ● Local history section ● Information desk	● Books to borrow. Magazines and newspapers ● Local guides to recyling depots, council departments and local tips ● Photographs of local shops and people. Local documents, tapes of local people talking ● Information on the local history society. Information on how to further your research, useful addresses and additional reference material
Yellow Pages	Local waste disposal, recycling, scrap metal dealers and second-hand dealers	Information about their work and business
Local records office or county archives	Medical officers' reports, old trade directories, details of refuse collection and disposal at the turn of the century	Trade directories. Council health reports
Local history society	Your area a hundred years ago	Information, reference material, and advice on how to further your research

Places to visit

The following museums have reconstructed shops displaying original packaging and old advertisements, craft workshops or reconstructed rooms showing how people lived:

Beamish North of England Open Air Museum, Beamish Hall, Stanley, County Durham. Tel: 0207 231811
Brewhouse Yard Museum, Castle Boulevard, Nottingham NG1 1FB. Tel: 0602 483504
Castle Museum, Clifford Street, York YO1 1RY. Tel: 0904 653611
Elvaston Castle Museum, The Working Estate, Elvaston Castle Country Estate, Borrowash Lane, Elvaston, Derbyshire DE7 3EW. Tel: 0332 71342
Lincolnshire Life Museum, The Old Barracks, Burton Road, Lincoln LN1 3LY. Tel: 0522 28448
Luton Museum and Art Gallery, Wardown Park, Luton, Beds, LU2 7HA. Tel: 0582 36941
Market Harborough Museum, Council Offices, Adam and Eve Street, Market Harborough, Leicestershire.
Museum of East Anglian Life, Stowmarket, Suffolk IP14 1DL Tel: 0449 612229
North Holderness Museum of Village Life, 11, Newbegin, Hornsea, North Humberside HU18 1DB. Tel: 04012 3443
People's Palace, Glasgow Green, Glasgow G40 1AT. Tel: 041 554 0223
Robert Opie Collection Museum of Packaging and Advertising, Albert Warehouse, Gloucester Docks, Gloucester GL1 2EH. Tel: 0452 302309.
Tredegar House and Country House, Tredegar House, Newport, Wales NP1 9YW. Tel: 0633 62275
Welsh Folk Museum, St. Fagans, Cardiff CF5 6XB. Tel: 0222 569441

The following natural history museums have information or displays about natural scavengers and vermin:
Natural History Museum, Cromwell Road, London SW7 5BD. Tel: 071 589 6323
Natural History Museum, Wollaton Hall, Wollaton Park, Nottingham NG8 2AE. Tel: 0602 281333 or 0602 281130

Useful addresses

Community Furniture Network, Highbank, Halton Street, Hyde, Cheshire SK14 2NY. Send SAE for local schemes of furniture re-use.
Friends of the Earth, 26–28 Underwood Street, London N1 7JQ. Send SAE
Rainbow Centre, 108 Mansfield Road, Nottingham (local resource directory, library)
Waste Watch, 26 Bedford Square, London WC1B 3HU (Send SAE for information and advice on recycling)

Who can tell you more?

They can. Use a tape recorder to record their memories. Label any items they loan you, look after them carefully and return them

Shopkeepers often know a lot about their stock and can answer questions. They may be able to give you names of local collectors to contact

• The curator or museum education officer. There may be leaflets or trails to help you

• The education department, the loans officer. Your teacher will have to arrange this
• The curator or education officer. Ask if there are talks or slide shows

• The librarian

The company may have an information officer. Write to them. Your teacher may be able to organise a visit

The archivist. Phone to find out how to use the archives. Documents are for reference only. Photocopies may be allowed by arrangement

The secretary

Index

Published by A & C Black (Publishers) Limited
35 Bedford Row
London WC1R 4JH
This edition © 1991 A & C Black (Publishers) Limited

ISBN 0 7136 3351 4

A CIP catalogue record for this book
is available from the British Library.

Apart from any fair dealing for the purposes of research or
private study, or criticism or review, as permitted under the
Copyright, Designs and Patents Act, 1988, this publication
may be reproduced, stored or transmitted, in any form or by
any means, only with the prior permission in writing of the
publishers, or in the case of reprographic reproduction in
accordance with the terms of licences issued by the Copyright
Licensing Agency. Inquiries concerning reproduction outside
those terms should be sent to the publishers at the above
named address.

Filmset by August Filmsetting, Haydock, St Helens
Printed in Italy by Amadeus

Acknowledgements

All photographs by Maggie Murray except for: p18, 27 (top
right) Mary Evans Picture Library; p19 (top), 26 (top) The
Greater London Photographic Library; p8 (bottom), 11
(bottom), 14 (top), and cover (inset) The Hulton Deutsch
Collection; p10 (bottom), 16 (top) Nottinghamshire Local
History Archive; p14 (bottom), 27 (bottom) Topham Picture
Library.

The cries of Old London from 'Speech Rhymes Book 1' Clive
Sanson, (A & C Black Ltd); extracts by Flora Klickman from her
book 'Mistress of the Little House' published in 1902.

The author and publisher would like to thank the following
people for their valuable help during the preparation of this
book: Suella Postles, Curator Brewhouse Yard Museum,
Nottingham; Don Sharp, taxidermist, Wollaton Hall Natural
History Museum; Jeremy Farrell, Pam Wood and all
Nottingham Museum staff; Peter Hammond, Phylis Norton;
Chris Latham, rush and cane chair restorer, Cotgrave, Notts;
June Dickenson, Rags and Riches, Nottingham; Gillian Clarke,
Anne Marie Button, and especially Jenny, Marcus and Laura